essential careers™

DENTAL HYGIENIST

Ann Byers

ROSEN
PUBLISHING®

NEW YORK

Published in 2013 by The Rosen Publishing Group, Inc.
29 East 21st Street, New York, NY 10010

First Edition

Library of Congress Cataloging-in-Publication Data

Byers, Ann.
A career as a dental hygienist/Ann Byers.—1st ed.
     p. cm.—(Essential careers)
Includes bibliographical references and index.
ISBN 978-1-4488-8235-9 (library binding)
1. Dental hygienists—Vocational guidance—Juvenile literature. 2. Dental hygiene—Vocational guidance—Juvenile literature. 3. Teeth—Care and hygiene—Juvenile literature. I. Title.
RK60.5.B94 2013
617.6'01023—dc23

                                                                    2012010618

Manufactured in the United States of America

CPSIA Compliance Information: Batch #W13YA: For further information, contact Rosen Publishing, New York, New York, at 1-800-237-9932.

contents

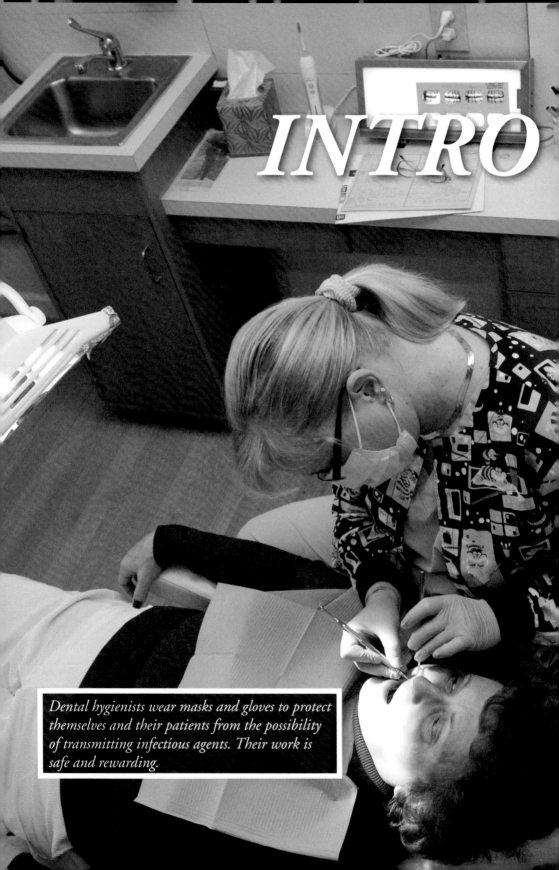

INTRO

Dental hygienists wear masks and gloves to protect themselves and their patients from the possibility of transmitting infectious agents. Their work is safe and rewarding.

DUCTION

Judy Boothby had been told that the elderly woman was "difficult." She was always angry and seemed uncomfortable around people. She did not want anyone poking around in her mouth. But Boothby was not afraid of difficult patients. In her job as a dental hygienist, she worked mainly with older people. Most of her patients lived in nursing homes or assisted living apartments.

Even though the woman did not want to see a dental hygienist, Boothby started visiting her. She found out why the woman stayed in her room all the time and why she was so unhappy. She did not like the way she looked. She had only a few teeth, and several of them were broken. Others were decaying. She had dentures—false teeth—that did not fit right. She was embarrassed to open her mouth in front of people. Because her teeth were broken, she could not eat normal food; she had to have everything mashed up. In addition, the decay caused infections, bleeding, and pain. A dental hygienist was exactly what this miserable, lonely woman needed!

Boothby convinced the woman to let her help. She cleaned her teeth and got rid of all the infection. She removed the decay and put temporary fillings in. She made arrangements for her to go to a dentist, who fixed the broken teeth and got her dentures to fit nicely.

These improvements in the woman's dental health brought huge changes in her life. She began going to the dining room and taking part in the home's activities. She talked and laughed with others. She ate better, so her overall health improved. She paid attention to her clothes and started wearing makeup. This difficult woman became a happy, friendly, and well-liked resident of her nursing home.

This woman's experience is one of the reasons why Boothby enjoys being a dental hygienist: she knows she is making a big difference in her patients' lives. She helps people correct problems and stay healthy. She spots small problems before they become big, and she refers her patients to dentists if they need treatment. She helps them feel and look their best.

A career as a dental hygienist can be very rewarding. In a survey of more than five thousand hygienists, almost 90 percent were happy with their jobs, according to the American Dental Hygienists' Association. In addition to keeping their patients healthy, many dental hygienists form relationships with the people they serve. They often get to know their patients over several years. Sometimes they treat entire families.

Most hygienists work in dental offices. The offices are usually very nice with top-quality, up-to-date equipment. A few practice in doctors' offices, health clinics, hospitals, and other health care settings. Some work in schools, in prisons, on military bases, or on Indian reservations. Hygienists work alongside dentists and dental assistants.

Dental hygiene is a very flexible career choice. Hygienists can choose to work full-time or part-time. They can often arrange their work hours to fit their scheduling needs. Because hygienists go to school to become certified and they develop special skills, they are paid well. Another great benefit of a career as a dental hygienist is the fact that the job will always be needed.

chapter 1

THE JOB

Because "hygienic" means "clean" or "sanitary," people usually think a dental hygienist's job is to clean teeth. But cleaning teeth is only one part of the job. A dental hygienist also examines patients, teaches them, and sometimes treats their problems. The job of dental hygienists can be summarized in one phrase: help people have healthy mouths.

PATIENT EVALUATION

A healthy mouth is more than shiny teeth. A healthy mouth involves everything in and around the mouth: teeth, gums, tongue, jawbone, and all the tissue inside the mouth. A hygienist is concerned not only with dental (teeth) health, but also with oral (mouth) health.

Oral health affects a person's overall well-being because the parts of the body are connected. Bacteria that live in the mouth can get into the bloodstream. These bacteria may be harmless in the mouth but can cause problems in other places. And diseases in other parts of the body can show up in the mouth. For example, diabetes can cause dry mouth. So dental hygienists examine their patients.

They usually ask questions about patients' medical history. They find out if they are taking any medications. Sometimes they take the patient's temperature, blood pressure, and pulse. They simply want to make sure that whatever they do for

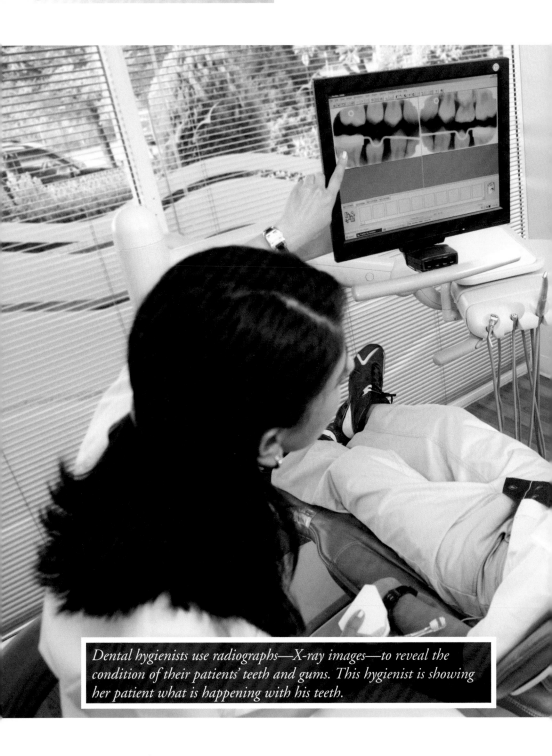

Dental hygienists use radiographs—X-ray images—to reveal the condition of their patients' teeth and gums. This hygienist is showing her patient what is happening with his teeth.

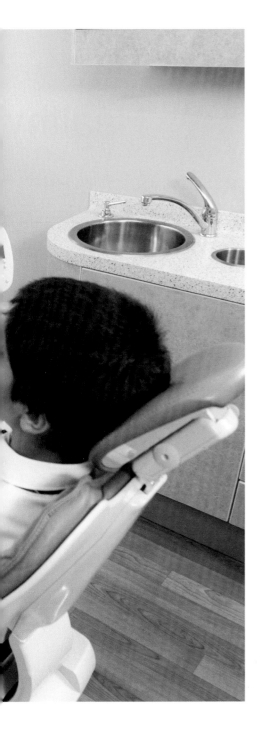

the patient does not interfere with any condition the patient may have.

When hygienists examine their patients' mouths, they look for more than evidence of decay or other problems with their teeth. They see if the gums are healthy—pink and tight around the teeth—or red and puffy. They may wiggle the teeth to check how firm the gums are. They look carefully for sores, lumps, and anything abnormal. These could signal an infection. Feeling under a patient's chin tells the hygienist if lymph nodes are healthy. Swelling or tenderness in this area can be signs of throat or oral cancer. For more detailed examination, hygienists take radiographs (X-rays) of their patients' teeth.

PREVENTIVE DENTAL CARE

After evaluating their patients' health, hygienists provide preventive dental care. Preventive care prevents, or stops, problems with teeth. Most tooth problems begin with cavities, and cavities begin with plaque.

Dental plaque is a soft, thin film that attaches itself to teeth. It is made up of microscopic bits of food, mucus, and dead cells from inside the mouth. Bacteria also live in plaque, feeding on sugars in food. The bacteria in plaque produce acids and toxins (poisons). The acids eat into enamel, the hard coating that covers the teeth. This is what makes cavities and tooth decay. The toxins attack the gums and, over time, they can cause periodontal (gum) disease.

If the soft plaque stays on the teeth for more than a day, it combines with minerals in the mouth to form tartar, also called calculus. Tartar often looks yellow or brown. It is hard and rough—just right for the sticky plaque with all its bacteria.

Plaque can be removed by proper brushing and

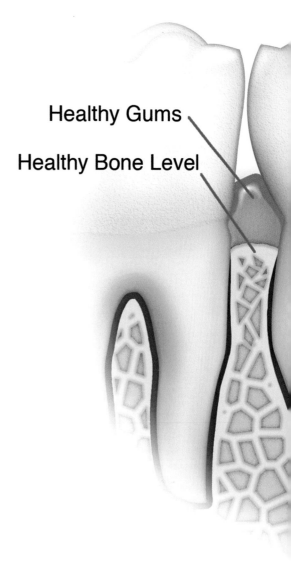

Healthy

Healthy Gums

Healthy Bone Level

Periodontal Disease

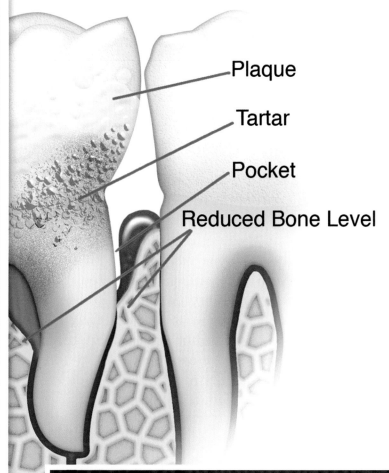

Plaque

Tartar

Pocket

Reduced Bone Level

This picture from a health textbook illustrates the difference between plaque and tartar and shows how these substances, when left on the teeth, affect the gum and bone.

flossing, but tartar cannot. Tartar has to be scraped off. It must be removed carefully with special tools so that the scraping does not damage the teeth. Dental hygienists are trained to clean both plaque and tartar off teeth. In this way they help their patients prevent cavities, decay, and gum disease.

Another way hygienists provide preventive dental care is by applying fluoride and sealants to children's teeth. Fluoride strengthens teeth, making decay less likely. Sealants are plastic coatings that fill the pits or grooves that are in some teeth. The pits are hard to clean with simple brushing, but the plastic seals them so that no bacteria can get in.

EDUCATION

The best preventive care in a dental office cannot replace good home care. A hygienist can help people have healthy mouths by teaching them how to care for their own teeth and gums. Education is an important part of the hygienist's job.

Hygienists show their patients the most effective ways to brush and floss. They explain the differences in toothbrushes, pastes, and gels and help their patients decide which products are best for them. They show their patients various tools for keeping their mouths healthy, and they demonstrate how to use them. Hygienists also explain how what people put in their mouths—foods, cigarettes, chewing gum—affects their oral health. They encourage people to choose healthy foods and healthy habits. Some dental hygienists go to schools, libraries, and community events to promote good oral practices.

SIMPLE DENTAL PROCEDURES

In general, hygienists provide preventive dental services and dentists provide therapeutic services. Therapeutic services are procedures aimed at healing. In other words, hygienists work

HOW IT ALL STARTED

At one time, people went to the dentist only when their teeth hurt. Nearly everyone had a toothache at some time because no one knew how to take care of their oral health. All dentists did was pull teeth, put caps on broken ones, and make false teeth to replace the ones they pulled. But a Connecticut dentist, Alfred Fones, thought he knew why people's teeth went bad and why their gums hurt: they were covered with plaque and tartar. He tried to tell other dentists and doctors that if people would clean their teeth, their mouths would feel better and their teeth would last longer. But in 1906, no one believed him. Other doctors did not see the value of preventive care.

So Dr. Fones set out to prove his theory. He used some of the teeth he had pulled from his patients to make a model of a mouth. He put plaster of Paris around the base of the teeth to look and feel like tartar and stains. Then he taught his cousin, Irene Newman, how to clean the teeth.

Before long, other dentists saw that Dr. Fones's patients had healthier mouths than their patients. When Dr. Fones opened his first School of Dental Hygiene in 1913, dental professors from Harvard, Yale, and other well-known universities volunteered to teach. In the first year, twenty-seven students graduated. A new career was born: that of dental hygienist.

on healthy mouths and dentists work on diseases or other dental problems. But in some places, hygienists perform some simple therapeutic procedures.

Hygienists may do root planing and scaling. These are deep cleanings that remove plaque and tartar from the lower portions of the teeth, the parts below the gum line, around the tooth roots. Scaling scrapes away bacteria and toxins; root planing smoothes the surface of the root so that bacteria do not stick as well. People with gum problems often need to have such deep cleaning.

Each U.S. state has its own rules about what dental hygienists are allowed to do. In some states, they can mix the materials for fillings and put them in patients' teeth. In other states, they can put in temporary fillings, but only a dentist can insert permanent fillings. Some hygienists can give their patients anesthetics. Hygienists sometimes assist dentists when they perform oral surgery. Although they cannot perform any part of the surgery, some hygienists can take out the stitches after the surgery is over.

OTHER RESPONSIBILITIES

In addition to direct work with patients, hygienists must prepare for each patient's visit. They have to sharpen and sterilize their instruments, and they have to clean their equipment and workspace. They must carefully record each patient's condition and progress. Keeping patients' charts up-to-date is an important part of their job.

Thus, a dental hygienist is part cleaner, part dentist, part technician, part teacher, and part record keeper. It is quite an interesting job!

chapter 2

CAREER OPTIONS

Just as a hygienist's job is much more than cleaning teeth, the careers open to hygienists go far beyond working in a dental office. The American Dental Hygienists' Association lists five career paths for dental hygienists: clinician, teacher, researcher, manager, and advocate. Each has the same purpose: help people have healthy mouths.

CLINICIAN

Every hygienist begins in the role of clinician. A clinician is a person who practices some form of healing, a person directly involved in helping people get well or stay well. Before hygienists can follow any other career path, they must thoroughly understand dental hygiene. They have to have practice evaluating patients, providing preventive care, teaching patients about oral health, and perhaps performing some basic therapeutic procedures.

The vast majority of hygienists remain in the career of clinician. They enjoy working directly with people. After all, most became hygienists because they wanted to help people. More than 95 percent of all hygienists in the United States are clinicians in dental offices, according to the American Dental Hygienists' Association. But dental offices are not the only places dental clinicians can work. Hygienists are needed in

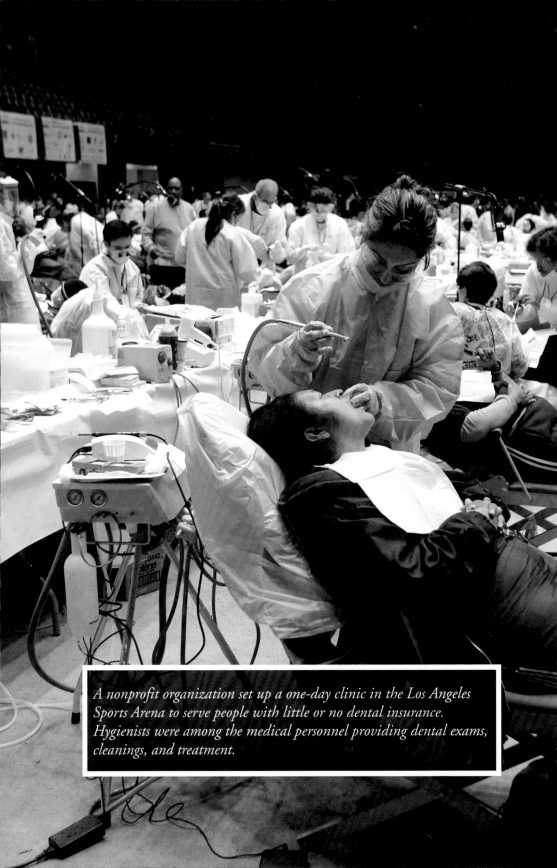

A nonprofit organization set up a one-day clinic in the Los Angeles Sports Arena to serve people with little or no dental insurance. Hygienists were among the medical personnel providing dental exams, cleanings, and treatment.

some doctors' offices and hospitals. All these hygienists work in private practice, which means patients pay them either directly or through insurance.

Some hygienists work in community settings. Community settings are schools, clinics, prisons and juvenile halls, homes for the elderly or disabled, military bases, and Indian reservations. Each of these is its own little community. In community settings, hygienists are paid not by their patients, but by government agencies or nonprofit groups. Patients in community settings often cannot afford to pay for oral health care. Community-based dental service is called public health dentistry to distinguish it from private practice dentistry.

Hygienists in public dental health think of the community as their patient, rather than just the individuals in the community. So in addition to the normal clinician duties, public health hygienists do outreach and dental health screenings. Outreach is going out into the community, talking to people about oral health and persuading them to come in to the clinic to receive care. Screening is examining people to see what their dental needs are. Many hygienists who work in community settings are especially happy that they are able to teach and help people who would not have dental care without them.

TEACHER

Hygienists who want to teach have a number of career options. One is in public schools. Hygienists can teach children how to care for their teeth as early as preschool. In elementary school, they can also explain the connection between what people eat and their oral health. In the upper grades, dental hygiene is often a part of science or health class. Some high schools have vocational courses that prepare students for jobs. Others have programs that introduce students to different careers. Either of these is a great opportunity for a hygienist educator.

Another opportunity is in training hygienists. Community colleges, technical colleges, dental schools, and four-year colleges

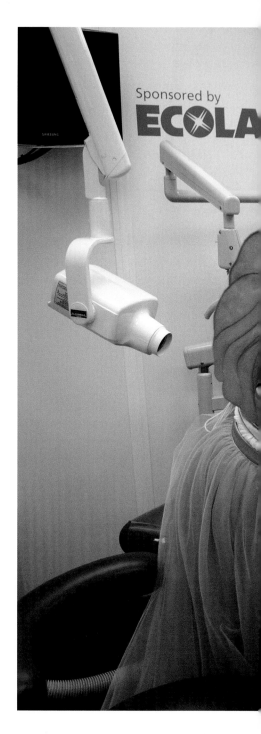

Sponsored by
ECOLA

A dental hygienist at a mobile dental clinic acts as a "tooth fairy" to help children relax in order to permit hygienists and dentists to give them oral care.

have programs that prepare people to become dental hygienists. Most also have continuing education classes that enable hygienists to stay up on the latest techniques.

Community settings have many needs for dental educators. Clinics often hire hygienists to conduct classes or seminars on dental health. Clinics and community organizations frequently have hygienists speak or demonstrate good oral care at health fairs and other neighborhood events.

Dental education is not all lecture and classroom instruction. Sometimes it is using a puppet, or singing songs, or even dressing up as "Myrtle the Molar." Many hygienists who choose the education career path teach only part-time; the rest of the time they work as clinicians or in other jobs in the field.

RESEARCHER

One other job option for educators and hygienists is research. Dentists and people who make dental equipment and materials do research to make their practice and instruments better. Dental sealants, electric toothbrushes, and fluoride toothpaste are all the results of research. Two types of research for dental hygienists are clinical research and product development.

Clinical research has to do with everyday practices of oral health. Clinical researchers study the effects of foods, medicines, and diseases on teeth and gums. They look for ways to improve the techniques clinicians use. They try to discover the early signs of oral cancer and gum disease. Other researchers design equipment, appliances, drugs, and other products that make it easier for dentists and hygienists to do their jobs and for ordinary people to take good care of their oral health.

Dental research takes teams of people. For example, consider a simple study on whether Toothbrush A cleans teeth better than Toothbrush B. Someone has to design the study, and someone has to find people to be in it—lots of people.

Scientists think chewing gum made of decapeptide (KSL) can fight plaque and tartar buildup on teeth. KSL keeps the microbes that form plaque from growing. These samples are being developed for soldiers in combat zones who cannot always brush their teeth twice a day.

Someone has to distribute the toothbrushes and make sure that everyone is using them the same way. People are needed to record the results, analyze them, and figure out what they mean. And this is a simple study!

Hygienists can find research opportunities at government agencies, health care companies, and businesses that manufacture health care products. Some universities have research departments. Hygienists working as clinicians or educators can also participate in research.

MANAGER, CONSULTANT, ADVOCATE

Once hygienists master the clinical aspects of the job, some earn a master's degree that opens up other career paths. If they have skills in administration—in running things—they can manage a dental office. As managers, they take charge of scheduling, hiring, and day-to-day operations. Hygienists might work as clinicians or educators in a clinic or another community program and eventually become the manager of the program.

Several options are available to hygienists as managers and consultants in companies that make dental products. They might advise the people developing the products because they understand how the products will affect both clinicians and their patients. They could manage the public relations department because they are comfortable talking with dentists and hygienists. Some manage sales departments, helping salespeople learn how to present the products. They also make good salespeople for companies that make oral care products.

Whatever career path they choose, many hygienists naturally become advocates for good oral health. They know the importance of oral health and they know how to achieve it. So they automatically encourage others to brush and floss properly, visit their dentist regularly, and follow a healthy

TONYA RAY, CLINICIAN, EDUCATOR, AND MANAGER

Tonya Ray has traveled three different paths in her career as a dental hygienist. She began as a clinician in a school for people with developmental disabilities. She really enjoyed knowing that she was helping her patients. Then she went back to school and became a teacher. She loved helping others become dental hygienists. While she was teaching, she also managed the school's dental clinic. After that, she became a manager for large companies that made dental products. She travels all over the country, using her skills as a hygienist as she meets people, trains them, and helps their businesses grow. Every job has brought new challenges and new rewards. And she has loved every one of them.

diet. Some become professional advocates. They work mainly in public health as patient advocates. Advocates help people recognize their health needs and work with them to meet those needs. They give them the education and connect them with the resources that will enable them to practice good oral health care. In some communities, patients have difficulty knowing how and where to get what they need. Advocates help them understand and access all that is available. Dental health care advocacy is very rewarding for hygienists who like helping people.

FORENSICS

One lesser known career path for the dental hygienist is that of forensics. Forensic dentistry uses knowledge of teeth as legal

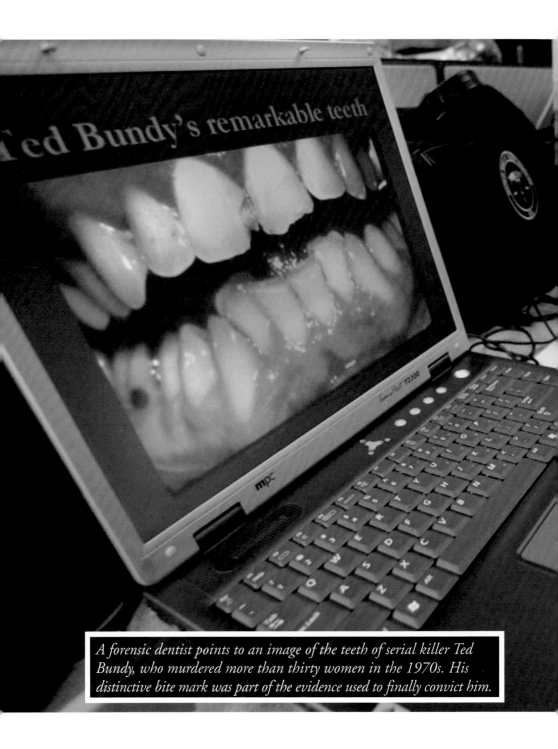

A forensic dentist points to an image of the teeth of serial killer Ted Bundy, who murdered more than thirty women in the 1970s. His distinctive bite mark was part of the evidence used to finally convict him.

evidence. Forensic dentistry teams generally do two things: (1) they use dental information to identify a body, and (2) they match bite marks with teeth to find out who did the biting. A forensic dentist can tell a lot about people by examining their teeth: how old they are, whether they are male or female, and what their race is. Sometimes they can tell if they were wealthy or poor, if they smoked, or if they took certain medicines or had certain diseases. Usually they identify people by comparing their dental records with the physical evidence they find. Forensic dental teams have been invaluable in identifying victims of natural disasters such as hurricanes and tsunamis, identifying crime victims, and even uncovering criminals.

Hygienists make good members of forensic teams. They are used to spotting unusual traits in people's teeth. They are skilled in taking and understanding radiographs. They are accustomed to noticing and recording the tiniest details about their patients' teeth. Many hygienists who serve on forensic teams also work as clinicians, teachers, managers, or consultants.

A Flexible Career

The field of dental hygiene has many different job options. Hygienists can work full-time or part-time. They can work days or nights, weekdays or weekends. They can divide their time between different types of jobs, such as clinician, teacher, and researcher. They can work in a small office with one dentist or in a large medical complex. They can specialize, caring for children, working for periodontists (those who treat gum conditions), or helping with oral surgery. They can choose private practice or public dental health. Dental hygiene is truly a flexible career choice!

chapter 3

WHAT IT TAKES

No matter which career path they choose, dental hygienists need to master a variety of instruments and equipment. Some are for diagnosing, or evaluating, patients' conditions; some are for cleaning teeth; and some are for keeping patients' mouths healthy.

PROBES

One of the first instruments a hygienist uses in an exam is a dental probe, or explorer. As the name suggests, its purpose is to probe, or explore, the teeth and gums to see what condition they are in. Probes are thin, straight instruments with sharp, hooked ends. Some probes have hooks on only one end, and some have two curved ends, one slightly larger than the other. The curve lets the hygienist slip the probe around and between teeth. The hygienist pokes the teeth with the sharp end to find any decay. Tooth decay begins as soft spots on the tooth's enamel, and the spots are too tiny to see in the beginning. But a trained hygienist can feel them with the probe.

Hygienists have to be very gentle when exploring teeth. If they are too rough, the sharp probe can turn a minor problem into a major one. Sometimes a slight bit of decay can be removed and the tooth repaired with a fluoride treatment, but harsh probing can widen a small hole in the enamel.

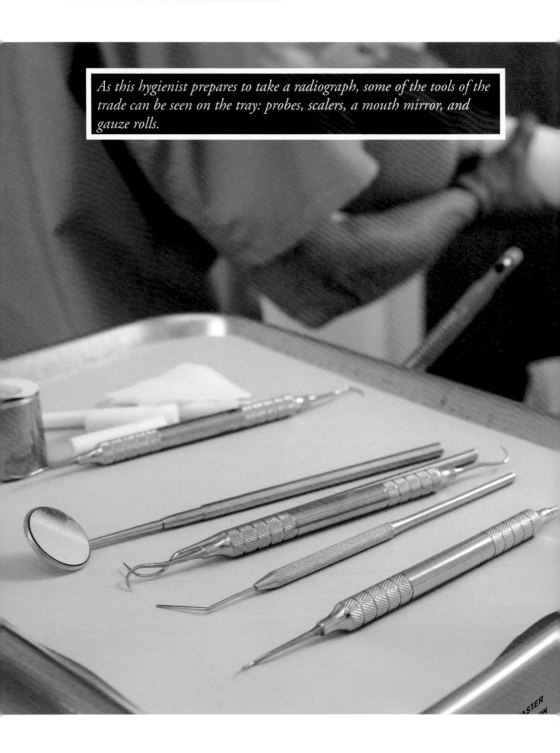

As this hygienist prepares to take a radiograph, some of the tools of the trade can be seen on the tray: probes, scalers, a mouth mirror, and gauze rolls.

The pointed end of the probe is also a measuring device. The hygienist uses it to measure the gum pocket—how far below the gum line the gum is separated from the teeth. This measurement tells how healthy the gums are.

RADIOGRAPHS

The best dental hygienist exploring with the finest dental probe can miss some problems. Some cavities are just too small to detect or located in places too difficult to reach. The hygienist cannot see what is happening inside the gums. To discover what they cannot see or feel with their instruments, hygienists take radiographs of their patients' mouths.

Radiographs used to be called X-rays. They are pictures of the insides of solid objects. Hygienists use them to spot any problems with their patients' teeth, gums, mouth, and jaw. They can show cavities, bone loss or damage, gum infections, and the positions of teeth that have not yet broken through the gums.

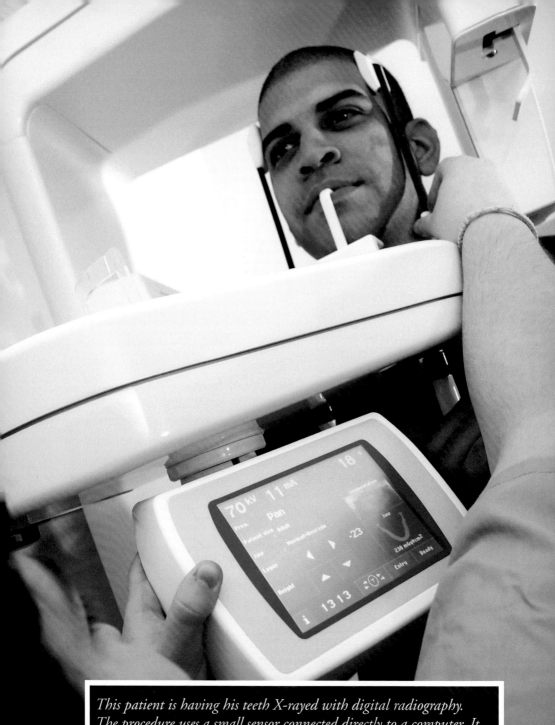

This patient is having his teeth X-rayed with digital radiography. The procedure uses a small sensor connected directly to a computer. It requires no film, no developing chemicals, and 80 percent less radiation than conventional radiography.

The radiograph machine uses a very small amount of radiation to produce images. Many dental offices today use a newer technology called digital radiography. Digital radiographs are taken, stored, and viewed with computers instead of film. Some hygienists prefer digital radiography because it uses less radiation.

Hygienists not only take and process radiographs of their patients; they also interpret them. Radiographs are basically images of light and dark. Hygienists look at the pictures and figure out what they mean. For example, a dark spot on a white background may indicate a cavity on a tooth. Hygienists might notice problems, but they are not licensed to actually diagnose them. They can point out their findings to a dentist and the dentist can treat the patient.

INVENTING HER OWN SOLUTION

A big challenge for dental hygienists is recording information about their patients' teeth. They need to write down what they see in their patients' mouths, but they also need to keep their hands clean. If they use a pen or a computer to record the information and then go back to working on the patient, germs on the equipment could be transferred to the patient. Dental hygienist Becky Logue solved the problem. She invented the Dental R.A.T. (Remote Access Terminal). The R.A.T. is a large computer mouse placed on the floor and operated with the foot. It allows hygienists to put information into their computers without stopping their dental work and contaminating their hands. Logue got the idea when she saw her children play a game on a dance pad. Today, hundreds of hygienists use her invention.

Dentists recommend that patients have radiographs taken regularly, at least every few years, depending on their patients' age and the condition of their oral health. The images taken at different times can reveal conditions that may need attention. Hygienists are often responsible for keeping records of their patients' radiographs and knowing when to take new ones. The records as well as the images themselves are important in the evaluation aspect of the dental hygienist's job.

SCALERS

After the evaluation comes the cleaning—removing the soft and hard deposits that build up on teeth. Cleaning tools are called scalers. Scalers look very much like probes, but their tips are very narrow triangular blades, rather than pointed ends. Hygienists use scalers to scrape plaque and tartar from teeth. They use different scalers—with their blades curved at various angles—so that they can reach teeth in different positions. When they clean below the gum line, they switch to curettes. A curette is a scaler with a rounded tip that is gentle against the gum.

These are all hand scalers. Hygienists may also use ultrasonic scalers. An ultrasonic scaler is a scaler that vibrates. Using an ultrasonic scaler is a little like using an electric toothbrush. The vibrations loosen built-up deposits faster than hand scaling. The hygienist removes the deposits by rinsing the teeth. Although they are faster and more comfortable for both patient and hygienist, ultrasonic scalers do not usually remove all tartar. Hygienists finish the cleaning with a hand scaler.

CLEANING AIDS

Probes and scalers are the primary instruments hygienists use, but other tools are also helpful. Specially designed mouth mirrors assist with probing. They enable the hygienist to see all the surfaces of any tooth and reflect light where it is needed. Hygienists also use mirrors to hold the patient's tongue or lip out of their way so that they can see the teeth better.

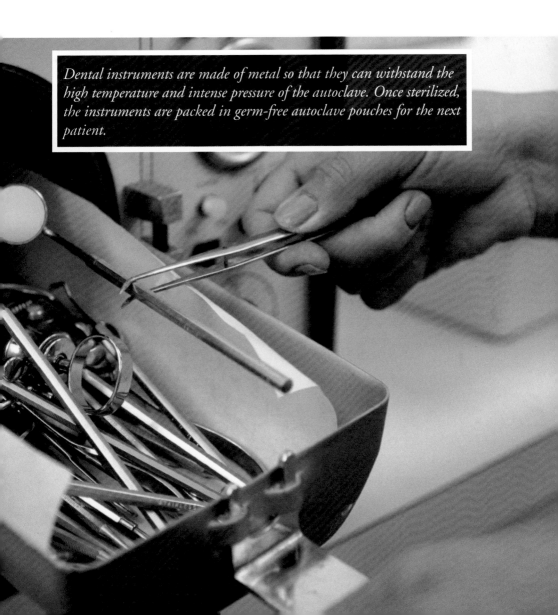

Dental instruments are made of metal so that they can withstand the high temperature and intense pressure of the autoclave. Once sterilized, the instruments are packed in germ-free autoclave pouches for the next patient.

As hygienists scrape plaque and tartar from their patients' teeth, they have to remove the debris. They use a water/air syringe for this purpose. The syringe shoots a blast of air, a stream of water, or both. The air and/or water flush the unwanted material away from the clean tooth.

But the debris has to go somewhere. So the hygienist uses a dental vacuum to suction it out of patients' mouths. The vacuum also removes blood and excess saliva. Sometimes a curved hose is attached to the vacuum and hooked loosely over the patient's lower lip. This allows hygienists to keep working on patients without having to stop frequently to suction their mouths.

After cleaning the teeth, the hygienist polishes them. The polish is applied with an electric instrument that rotates against the teeth. The purpose of polishing is not to make the teeth shine; it is to make them smooth so that it is more difficult for plaque to stick to them. After all, the hygienist's main job is not to make the patient look good, but to help the patient stay healthy.

Keeping patients healthy requires that hygienists do their jobs in a super-clean environment. That means they must sanitize their rooms between patients. They spray chairs, lights, trays, countertops, and hoses with a disinfectant. They wipe everything down and clean all their equipment. To make sure no bacteria remain, they sterilize their instruments in an autoclave. An autoclave uses steam under pressure to kill any contaminant.

PERSONAL ABILITIES

Operating these tools of the trade requires a certain amount of physical ability. Hygienists have

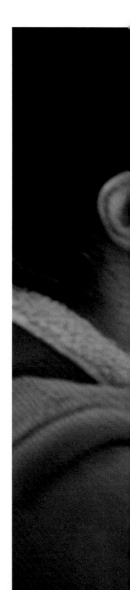

to have good finger dexterity. That is, they have to be able to hold small instruments in the fingers of one hand and move them carefully, gently, and firmly in tight spaces. They also have to have very good near vision. And they need to combine finger dexterity with good vision: the job demands excellent eye-hand coordination.

In addition to physical abilities, hygienists need people skills. Some people are nervous when they come to a dentist's office, and a hygienist is often the first clinician they see. The

Some dental hygienists use telescopic loupes to magnify their view of patients' mouths. The lights on these loupes are helpful because this hygienist is screening students in a school without the benefit of dental chairs and lights.

hygienist should be able to put patients at ease and make them feel comfortable. They need to listen to patients so that they can understand their needs. Because education is an important part of their job, they should also be able to explain things clearly.

Hygienists should be detail-oriented. That means they pay attention to small items. They not only have to notice tiny problems in their patients' mouths and slight differences on radiographs, but they also have to record much of what they see and do.

What's more, being a dental hygienist requires a great deal of knowledge and a number of technical skills. These are gained through professional training.

chapter 4

How to Get There

C leaning teeth and teaching people how to keep their mouths healthy may seem like a simple job, but it takes quite a bit of knowledge and skill. Dental hygienists have to understand the structures of the mouth and jaw. They have to know the relationship between oral health and the rest of the body. They need to know how diet and behavior affect teeth. They have to learn how to use all the tools of the trade. Moreover, they have to become good at it. Dental hygiene is a profession that requires education, practice, and a state license.

The first requirement is education. The American Dental Hygienists' Association recognizes three types of training programs: entry-level programs, degree completion programs, and master degree programs. In each type of program, students learn information and gain skills that enable them to qualify for different levels of dental hygienist jobs.

ENTRY-LEVEL TRAINING

Entry-level programs are exactly what the name suggests: they give students enough training to enter the profession. Every hygienist enters the profession as a clinician. To get a job as a dental hygienist, a person must graduate from a dental education program that is accredited, or approved, by the American Dental Association (ADA). The ADA sets the standards for

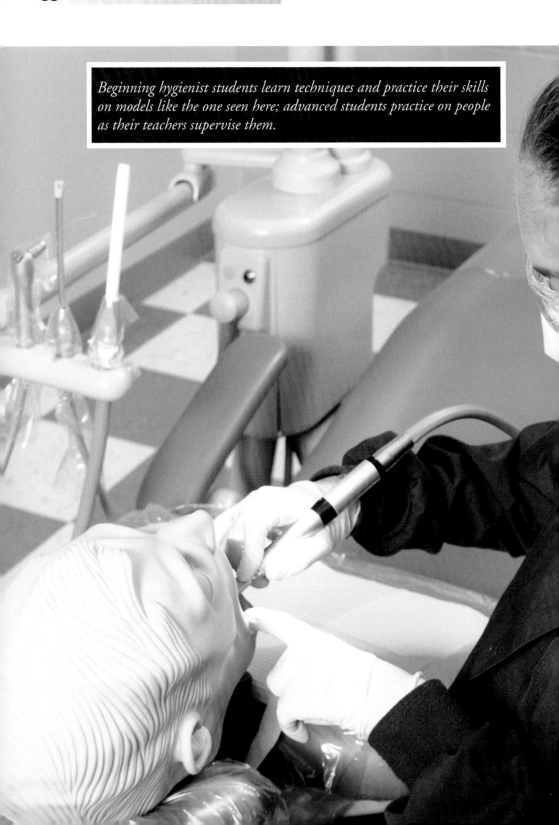

Beginning hygienist students learn techniques and practice their skills on models like the one seen here; advanced students practice on people as their teachers supervise them.

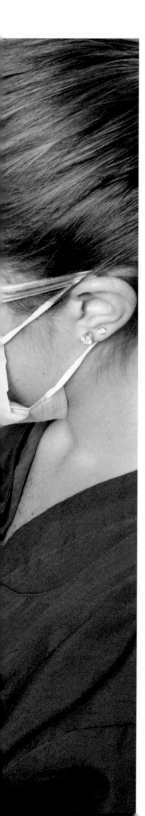

hygienist education for the entire nation. Entry-level programs grant three types of proof that a graduate is ready to practice dental hygiene: a certificate, an associate's degree, and a bachelor's degree.

The ADA has approved more than three hundred entry-level training programs in the United States. In the vast majority, students earn an associate's degree—an Associate of Arts (AA), Associate of Science (AS), or Associate of Applied Science (AAS). They are offered at community colleges, also called junior colleges; technical colleges; and dental schools. In a few programs, students earn a certificate instead of a degree.

Associate degree and certificate programs basically require two years of study. The student spends about 2,300 hours in the classroom and about 500 hours in hands-on practice. The classroom time includes general courses that all college students take, such as English, math, and sociology. It also includes science classes; hygienists must know something about chemistry, anatomy, microbiology, physiology, and nutrition. A person working in other people's mouths must also know quite a bit about dental science. So students in dental hygiene programs study the anatomy of the mouth and jaw and of the head and neck. They learn about teeth, gums, and diseases of the mouth. They learn how to manage pain, use different instruments, and take radiographs.

In the clinical portion of the program—the hands-on practice—the student performs services for real patients under the supervision of an instructor. Hygienist programs generally have their own clinics for this purpose. Often people in the community can schedule appointments at the training clinics and pay less than they would at a dental office. The services usually take longer because the students are learning. In addition to using the school's clinic, most programs also require their students to take some of their clinical hours in a public health setting.

With an associate's degree or a certificate, a graduate is prepared to work in a private dental office. People who want to work in public health or pursue other career paths need to have a bachelor's degree. Earning a bachelor's degree takes two additional years of study. Students in bachelor's programs take more classes in chemistry, health education, and counseling patients. They also have more hours of clinical practice. The extra training enables them to work in a community setting or as teachers or researchers.

DEGREE COMPLETION PROGRAMS

Most hygienists enter the field with a two-year degree or certificate. They may decide after working for a while that they want the skills and the opportunities a four-year degree offers. Hygienists with an associate's degree or a certificate can go back to school and earn a bachelor's degree. They do so by enrolling in a degree completion program. Fifty-seven schools have these programs. They allow a hygienist to obtain a Bachelor of Science degree in dental hygiene, health science, or allied health.

MASTER'S DEGREE PROGRAMS

Just as a bachelor's degree opens up more career options for the dental hygienist, a master's degree opens up even more. With a

Dr. Marie A. Collins, RDH, Ed.D., is chair of the Department of Dental Hygiene at the Medical College of Georgia School of Allied Health Sciences. The letters after her name identify her as a registered dental hygienist with a doctor's degree in education.

master's degree, a hygienist can train other clinicians, be in charge of clinics and other programs, and perform research. Graduates of master's degree programs often become managers or consultants. Throughout the country, only twenty schools

NATIONAL BOARD DENTAL HYGIENE EXAMINATION SAMPLE QUESTIONS

The virus responsible for which of the following diseases is the MOST resistant to chemical and physical agents?
  A. AIDS
  B. Herpes
  C. Measles
  D. Influenza
  E. Hepatitis

Periodontal disease is considered to be controlled when
  A. No bleeding on probing is present.
  B. The gingival tissue is firm, pink, and stippled.
  C. No pockets are deeper than 3 mm.
  D. Calculus and plaque have been removed.
  E. The gingival tissue height approximates the cementoenamel junction.

An antihistamine is the drug of choice for treating which of the following?
  A. Hay fever
  B. Common cold

offer the Master of Science degree in dental hygiene or a related subject. These programs have classes in research, leadership, and education, as well as in science topics.

C. Anaphylactic shock
D. Immune suppression
E. Vitamin C overdose

Each of the following characterizes an ideal chemical disinfectant EXCEPT one. Which one is this EXCEPTION?
A. Heat-stable
B. Long shelf-life
C. Water solubility
D. Activity against vegetative microbes
E. Activity against microbial spores

A 70-year-old edentulous patient routinely cleans and soaks her dentures in hot water. Which of the following can occur as a result of this practice?
A. Softening the base
B. Distorting the base
C. Loosening the teeth
D. Crazing the denture
E. Discoloring the denture

Answers: E, A, A, A, B

[Source: American Dental Association, National Board Dental Examinations, Sample Test (http://www.ada.org/sections/educationAndCareers/pdfs/nbdhe_ sample_test.pdf)]

STATE LICENSE

Education is only the beginning. The next step is obtaining a license. Education gives dental hygienists knowledge and skills; a license proves the knowledge and skills are good. Each state

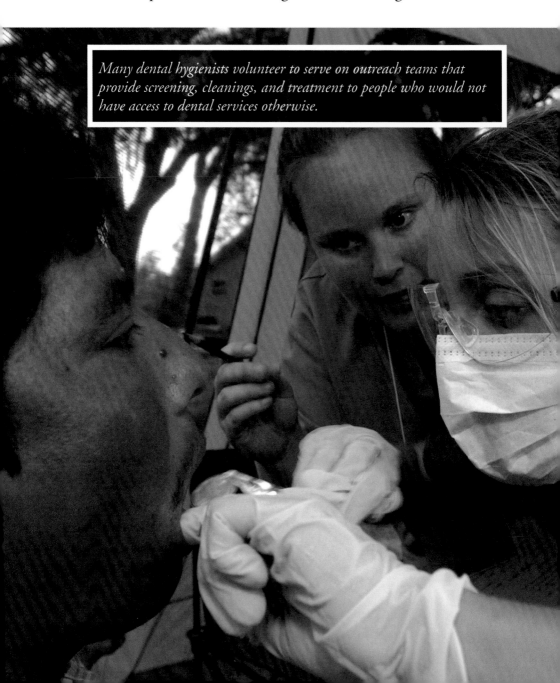

Many dental hygienists volunteer to serve on outreach teams that provide screening, cleanings, and treatment to people who would not have access to dental services otherwise.

has its own requirements for obtaining a license. A hygienist who is licensed in one state cannot practice in another without a license in that state also.

There are three steps to getting a license: graduation from an entry-level dental hygiene program and passing two exams.

One exam tests knowledge, and the other tests skills. The test of knowledge is a written test. Every state except Alabama uses the National Board Dental Hygiene examination designed by the ADA. Alabama has its own examination. The ADA exam is an eight-hour test. It is divided into two parts. The first part asks two hundred questions about basic science, oral health, hygienist practices, diseases of the mouth, dental materials, and other topics that hygienists should know. The second part gives scenarios that hygienists might encounter, and the test taker has to make decisions about patients' condition or treatment. There are no scores for the written test; it is graded as "pass" or "fail."

The test of skills—the clinical test—is a state test. Each state or group of states (region) has its own test. In the clinical test, test takers demonstrate their skills on real people. This test is also graded as "pass" or "fail." States may have additional requirements for obtaining a license. Many require hygienists to be certified in cardiopulmonary resuscitation (CPR). Some give tests on the legal aspects of the profession. Most states also require hygienists to have continuing education in order to keep their licenses. They must have a certain number of hours of training every year or two to keep their knowledge and skills current.

When all the requirements are met, dental hygienists proudly use the letters RDH after their names. These letters show that a person has completed at least two years of a very demanding training program and has passed two long and difficult tests. He or she is a registered dental hygienist.

chapter 5

CAREER PROSPECTS

Some people become dental hygienists because of the flexibility. They want to work part-time or particular hours. Some love science and medicine and want to work in that field. Others like to work with their hands in close spaces. Some choose the profession because dental hygienists make good money. Others like medicine or dentistry but want to go to school for only two years to start. Whatever the motivation, a lot of people select dental hygiene as a career.

The U.S. Bureau of Labor Statistics reported that there are more than 174,000 jobs for dental hygienists in the United States. But there are only 130,000 practicing hygienists. That is because about half of all hygienists work part-time. Many have more than one job, combining part-time positions to work full days. A number of them work as clinicians and as teachers, researchers, or in other career paths.

HIGH DEMAND

The Department of Labor estimates that even more hygienists will be needed in the years ahead. In fact, dental hygiene is one of the fastest-growing occupations in the country. The number of jobs that are expected to be needed in the next several years is rising at a rate of 36 percent each year. This means that thousands more hygienists will be required.

Carefully designed toothbrushes, scientifically formulated pastes and gels, and pleasantly flavored flosses encourage and enable people to practice good oral hygiene.

One reason the demand for hygienists is so high is that people are keeping their natural teeth longer than they used to. In years past, many people lost their teeth by the time they reached sixty, seventy, or eighty years of age. Most elderly people expected to have false teeth. Today, however, many people have most of their natural teeth all their lives.

The reason more people keep their teeth so long is that they understand the importance of preventive dental care. They are having their teeth cleaned twice each year. They are brushing and flossing properly. They have learned how to take care of their teeth, and they are doing a better job of it. Insurance companies are recognizing that preventing tooth and gum problems saves money, so more companies are offering better insurance. That means that more people are able to afford the type of care dental hygienists offer.

New tools and materials are helping people practice better oral hygiene. Fluorides and dental sealants help prevent cavities. Some electric toothbrushes are timed to help people brush for the right amount of time. New types of flosses, brushes, and stimulators enable people to massage their gums easily. Flavored pastes encourage

WHY GEORGE WASHINGTON NEVER SMILED

At age fifty, healthy adults have most of their thirty-two teeth. But at that age, George Washington probably had fewer than ten of his. Even though he brushed with tooth powder every day, used mouthwash, and saw a dentist, his mouth was in horrible shape. He lost his first tooth when he was only twenty-two, and by the time he became president, he had only one tooth left. His dentists made teeth for him out of ivory and other material (not wood!). The false teeth never fit well, and Washington was nearly always in pain. The missing teeth, ill-fitting dentures, and gum problems sometimes made his face look funny. Gilbert Stuart, who painted several famous portraits of the president, had him stuff his mouth with cotton so it would look more natural. No wonder there is no picture of George Washington smiling!

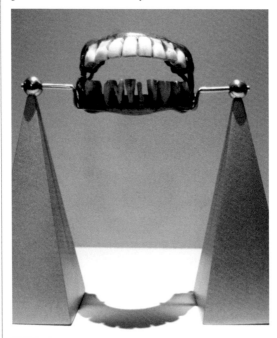

This is one of many sets of false teeth George Washington wore. The upper and lower dentures were held together with gold springs.

children to brush regularly. Modern radiographs and other equipment let dentists and hygienists detect and treat problems earlier. All these factors mean that more people have more teeth for more years . . . and more hygienists will be needed to help them care for those teeth.

MORE RESPONSIBILITIES

While the number of hygienists is rising, the number of dentists is not rising nearly as quickly. The number of dentists is not keeping pace with the number that is needed. In other words, demand for dentists is rising but supply is not going up at the same rate. So the workload of most dentists is increasing. Many dentists are asking their hygienists to perform some of

Dental hygienists study to become dental therapists. In the United States, only Minnesota and Alaska license dental therapists, who can do more than hygienists but less than dentists.

the tasks the dentists normally do. They are having hygienists administer anesthesia and take out stitches the dentists put in. Hygienists sometimes put fillings in patients' teeth, and sometimes they smooth and polish crowns and bridges.

Some states permit hygienists to do these additional tasks, and some do not. States may have to change their licensing rules to allow hygienists to assume the new roles. If hygienists are to have more responsibilities, they will need more education. The American Dental Hygienists' Association is exploring the possibility of having a new type of hygienist position: advanced dental hygiene practitioner (ADHP). The advanced hygienist would have additional training and be able to perform more procedures than the registered hygienist. An ADHP may also be able to practice without the direct supervision of a dentist.

CAREER TRACKS AND PATHS

The ADHP is one possible career path for a dental hygienist. A

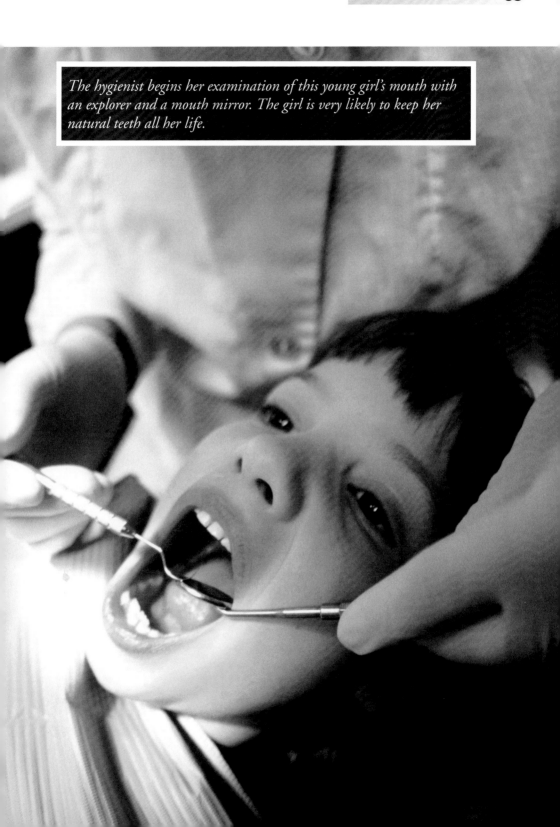

The hygienist begins her examination of this young girl's mouth with an explorer and a mouth mirror. The girl is very likely to keep her natural teeth all her life.

similar path created by the drop in the supply of dentists is the registered dental hygienist in alternative practice (RDHAP). Currently this position is offered only in California. Hygienists with this certification can work in nursing homes and other care facilities, schools, and homes of people who cannot leave their houses. They can work in areas where there are not enough dentists. They do not need a dentist's supervision, but if they serve one patient for more than eighteen months, that patient has to get a prescription from a dentist authorizing more treatment. About two hundred hygienists have RDHAP certificates.

Alternative practice, even in California, is rare. About 96 percent of all hygienists work in dental offices. Some work with general dentists, who see all kinds of patients, and some work with specialty dentists. The most common specialty practice for hygienists is periodontics, which deals with the gums. Another popular specialty is pediodontics, or children's dentistry. Some hygienists work with orthodontists, who straighten teeth and put on braces. Others enjoy oral surgery, and still others work with cosmetic dentists, who are concerned with the appearance rather than the health of their patients' teeth and mouths.

All of these career paths involve clinical practice. The non-clinical jobs described in chapter 2 are also good careers for hygienists—in education, research, management, consulting, and forensics. The demand for hygienists in public health is growing. Many hygienists find a career in public health particularly rewarding for a number of reasons. Working in a community setting gives them the opportunity to do clinical work and education at the same time. It often requires less direct supervision. Public health hygienists usually work with a variety of people, both coworkers and patients. And they can often see that they are making a big difference in people's lives.

Nearly half of all hygienists volunteer some of their time in public health, usually in schools or community health fairs.

PLUSES AND MINUSES

As with every career, there are positives and negatives to being a dental hygienist. For every plus there is a minus, and for every negative there is a positive. One of the biggest benefits of this career is its flexibility. Many mothers go into the profession because they want to work around their children's school schedules. They want to work only four or six hours a day, or they want to work evenings or weekends. The downside of the flexibility is that employees who work fewer than forty hours every week may not receive benefits. They may not have health insurance, paid vacation, or paid time off when they are sick. Furthermore, hygienists who want full-time work sometimes have a hard time finding it. Some employers would rather pay two part-time hygienists instead of one full-time one because they don't have to pay for benefits for part-time employees. So hygienists might have to juggle more than one job.

One lure that draws many to this profession is its good pay. For more information about the average salary for a full-time dental hygienist, check out the Bureau of Labor Statistics Web site (http://www.bls.gov). The income potential is especially high considering the short amount of time needed to qualify for the job. An entry-level position requires only a two-year degree. But with the likelihood of high pay comes competition. Many people are trying to get into dental hygienist training programs, but there are not enough programs for all the people who want them. Only a quarter of students trying to get into a two-year program and a third of those applying for a four-year program are admitted. So getting the training to test for a license is becoming harder than it once was.

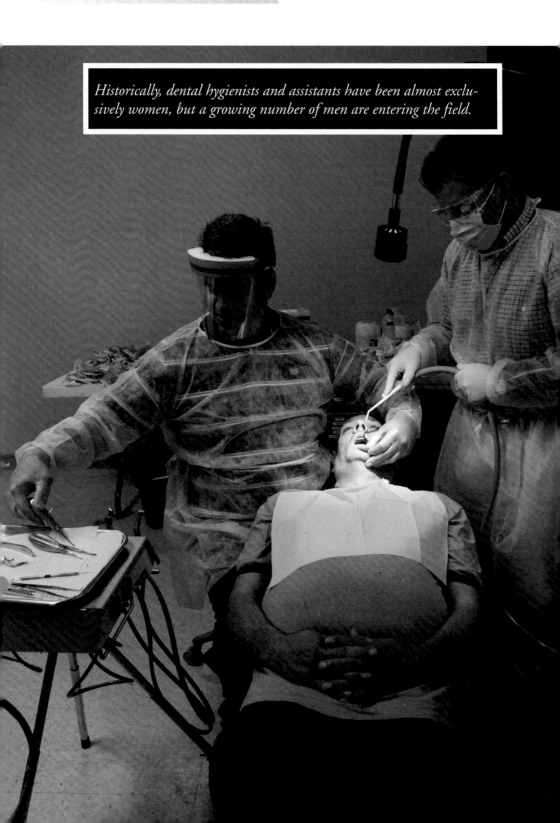

Historically, dental hygienists and assistants have been almost exclusively women, but a growing number of men are entering the field.

After people earn their RDH license, they might find competition in looking for a job, even though the need for hygienists is growing. The reason is that some areas of the country have lots of training programs—and therefore lots of graduates looking for work—and some have fewer. A hygienist who decides to move to where the jobs are runs into a problem if the jobs are in a different state. An RDH with a license in one state has to go through the clinical test in the second state to get a job there. Sometimes the second license has other requirements also, such as additional hours in training or practice.

Women especially find the flexibility and relatively high pay appealing. But this creates a negative for men. Dental hygiene is largely a female field; 99 percent of hygienists are women, according to the American Dental Hygienists' Association. There is no reason a man should not make a great hygienist. In fact, the few dentists who have hired male hygienists are quite pleased with them. Still, only a handful of men become hygienists. Many are probably reluctant to enter a profession that most people see as women's work.

Despite the few minuses, all the pluses make a career as a dental hygienist a great choice. In light of industry growth, stability, salary, and job satisfaction, *U.S. News and World Report* rated dental hygienist as one of the fifty best jobs in the country!

chapter 6

GETTING STARTED

I f you are thinking of dental hygiene as a career, it is not too early to begin planning. Actually, the planning process may help you decide if this is the right direction for you. The basic steps in pursuing a career in dental hygiene are the same as for achieving any important goal: assess your aptitude, gather all the information you can, develop a plan, and work your plan.

ASSESS YOUR APTITUDE

Assessing your aptitude means finding out if the job is something you would actually enjoy. Would you be happy spending hours doing the kinds of things dental hygienists do? Do you like science and medicine? Does working on other people's teeth and mouths sound interesting to you? Are you comfortable with all kinds of people? With being very close to them?

Ask yourself if you have what it takes to do the job. Can you sit or stand in one spot for a period of time, or do you need to move around? Can you work carefully with your hands and fingers, or do you prefer large-muscle activities? Can you do close-up work without straining your eyes? Do you pay attention to small details?

Most high schools, community colleges, and technical schools have career planning centers that can help you answer these questions. They have aptitude tests that let you know

Dental hygienists take impressions of patients' teeth, such as these shown here, to help make crowns, bridges, and other appliances that fit well and look natural.

what kind of work is a good fit for your personality. These tests are usually pretty accurate at steering people toward jobs they are likely to enjoy. You don't just want a job you can handle; you want a career you will love.

GATHER INFORMATION

If dental hygiene sounds like a good career for you, find out everything you can about the job. Reading this book is a great start. Read some of the books recommended at the end of this one. Talk to anyone you can find who works anywhere in the dental field. Talk with dentists, hygienists, dental assistants, and even receptionists in dental offices. Ask them what they like about their jobs and what they do not like. Ask if the job is what they thought it would be. If you can, talk with people in more than one office. Try to get a feel for what it would be like to work in a dental office. Is the atmosphere calm? Stressful? Enthusiastic? Do the employees seem happy?

There is nothing like seeing the actual job. You may think you know what a hygienist does because

HEALTH OCCUPATIONS APTITUDE EXAM SAMPLE QUESTIONS

Academic Aptitude

Sample A. a. Bad b. Evil c. Wicked d. Good e. Naughty
In the above set of words, which is most different in meaning from the other words?

Answer: d

Sample B. You have $10 and give $3 to your mother. How much do you have remaining?
a. $1 b. $2 c. $4 d. $5 e. $7

Answer: e

Sample C. ○ is to ○ as □ is to ___ ?
a. △
b. □
c. ▭
d. ○
e. ▯

Answer: b

1. Five health professionals earned the following scores on an anatomy test: 65, 82, 77, 89, 72. What is the average score?
a. 81 b. 78 c. 77 d. 72 e. 69

Answer: c

2. A 72-inch roll of bandage at $1.08 per yard would cost?
a. $1.08 b. $1.96 c. $2.16 d. $2.96 e. $3.24

Answer: c

Spelling
Each line below contains a word with three different spellings. Select the word from each line that is spelled correctly.
Sample A. a. acheive   b. achieve   c. achive
Answer: b
Sample B. a. emergancy   b. emergancie   c. emergency
Answer: c
Sample C. a. infectious   b. enfecteous   c. enfectious
Answer: a

Reading Comprehension
A few years ago, although no one knew it, the gases in spray cans were harming the ozone layer. The ozone layer is a part of the atmosphere, a thick blanket of air that covers the world. The atmosphere is made up of many gases, especially nitrogen and oxygen. Close to the earth, the atmosphere is thick and heavy, but as it gets farther away from the earth, the atmosphere gets thin. There, the energy from the sun changes the way gases behave. For example, oxygen atoms usually travel in the air connected together in pairs, but high in the atmosphere, the sun's energy causes three oxygen atoms to connect together instead of two. These groups of three oxygen atoms are called ozone. The place high in the air where regular oxygen changes to the ozone is called the ozone layer. The ozone layer is very important to life on earth. It soaks up dangerous rays from the sun that harm plants and animals. Even more important, the ozone layer helps keep the earth cool. Without it, the earth might become so hot that the ice caps would melt and flood much of the earth. Fortunately, safe gases are now used in spray cans, but some of the ozone layer has been destroyed.

(continued on page 64)

1. High in the sky the atmosphere is a. thick b. heavy c. unchanged d. thin
Answer: d
2. High in the atmosphere regular oxygen changes to a. solar rays b. oxygen rays c. ozone d. nitrogen
Answer: c
3. Without the ozone layer the earth would become a. cold b. hot c. dark d. frozen
Answer: b
4. The ozone layer serves to screen dangerous rays from a. oxygen atoms b. spray cans c. the sun d. the gases
Answer: c
5. The paragraph is chiefly concerned with the importance of the a. sun rays b. spray cans c. ice caps d. ozone layer
Answer: d

Information in the Natural Sciences
1. The lower jaw in vertebrates is known as the a. mandible b. hyoid c. pelvis d. coccyx e. ulna
Answer: a
2. In old age bones may become a. porous b. flexible c. ductile d. pliable e. supple
Answer: a
3. About one quart, 0.908 dry quart, is equivalent to one a. gram b. kilogram c. milligram d. calorie e. liter
Answer: e
4. Normal body temperature, expressed in degrees centigrade, is a. 212 b. 120 c. 98.6 d. 37 e. 22.8
Answer: d
5. The PH of a neutral solution is a. 0 b. 1 c. 5 d. 7 e. 10
Answer: d

[Source: Psychological Service Bureau, Sample Questions for the PSB Health Occupations Aptitude Examination, http://admin.psbtests.com/Uploads/Site Resources/11HOAEsq.pdf]

of your experience at the dentist's office. But your hygienist probably works on patients with dental situations far different from yours. Moreover, the hygienist has many responsibilities before and after your visit. Watching a hygienist at work for a few hours or a few days will give you a better idea of what the job involves. Some professionals permit people to shadow them, to follow them around as they work and observe them. See if your school's career planning center can make arrangements for you to shadow a hygienist or a dentist. Or ask your own dentist or hygienist.

Some organizations offer volunteer opportunities for people who are not skilled but are interested in health careers. Usually they are public health organizations that serve rural or low-income communities. Some help in disaster relief. You may simply assemble health care kits, pass out toothbrushes, clean and organize equipment, or entertain children as they wait for dental checkups. But you will be working alongside health care professionals, and that will give you a good feel for public health dentistry. It will also give you some experience that will make you stand out when you apply for admission to a hygienist training program. If the schools in your area are hard to get into, your hands-on experience may give you an edge over other applicants.

MAKE A PLAN

One piece of information you need to gather is what possibilities for training are available to you. What education programs are in your area? How much do they cost? What does it take to get into them?

Dental hygiene programs look at high school grade point average (GPA). You have to have at least a C average, and the higher the average, the better. You will need to have courses in math, biology, chemistry, and English—and good grades in

These students in a high school chemistry class are not only learning science but also building their résumés for future careers.

those classes. Programs also consider scores on college entrance tests such as the SAT. Again, the higher the score, the better your chances.

Usually you have to have some college before you will be accepted into a hygienist training program. Most programs want you to have about forty college units of chemistry, English, speech, psychology, and sociology. They look at your GPA in those classes and may pay special attention to your GPA in the science classes.

Many training programs require applicants to take an aptitude test before they will accept them into the program. The Health Occupations Aptitude Exam has five parts. Scores on the first four parts show whether people are ready for hygienist school. Part 1 measures the student's ability to learn. It includes vocabulary, math, and reasoning questions. Parts 2 and 3 test spelling and reading comprehension. Part 4 measures basic science knowledge. The last section has to do with attitudes, opinions, and other personality traits. It tells whether people are likely to do well in the profession.

WORK YOUR PLAN

The last step in getting started in a career as a dental hygienist is to work your plan. That means doing what it takes now to get into a good training program. Make sure you are taking the right courses in high school. Study hard to get good grades in those courses. Dental hygiene school is not cheap. You may need to be saving money now so that you can afford the education when you are ready.

If you have . . .

- taken a good, hard look at yourself
- and at what a career as a dental hygienist is like
- and you have decided this is probably the right path for you
- and you have checked out the training programs available to you
- and you are making yourself ready for those programs

. . . then you are well on your way to an exciting, rewarding future! Go for it!

glossary

accredited Authorized, or given approval, by a recognized organization.

ADHAP Advanced dental hygiene practitioner, a certification being considered that would create a hygienist position with more training and responsibilities than a registered dental hygienist.

advocate A person who helps someone with less power gain the ability to accomplish something specific; a person who publicly supports or recommends a particular cause or policy.

anatomy The science of the shape and structure of living beings or parts of living beings.

anesthetics Substances such as drugs that are used in medical or surgical procedures to induce insensitivity to pain.

autoclave Equipment that sterilizes items using pressurized steam.

calculus Also called tartar, a hard deposit that forms on teeth. It is composed of plaque and minerals, especially calcium.

clinician A person who practices one of the healing arts.

CPR Cardiopulmonary resuscitation, an emergency procedure used to help revive a person whose heartbeat and breathing have stopped.

curette A scaler with a rounded tip used for scaling below the gum line.

fluoride A compound that contains fluorine, a natural element that inhibits tooth decay.

GED General Education Diploma or General Equivalency Diploma, a credential earned by a person who did not graduate from high school that certifies that the person has passed tests showing that he or she has the same academic skills as someone who graduated from an American or Canadian high school.

periodontal Having to do with gums.

plaque A soft, sticky film that builds up on teeth. It is composed of food, bacteria, and other substances that occur naturally in the mouth.

RDH Registered dental hygienist, a certification given by the American Dental Hygienist Association showing that a person has completed all its requirements for practicing dental hygiene.

RDHAP Registered dental hygienist in alternative practice, a certification offered in California that allows a hygienist to practice in certain settings without the supervision of a dentist.

root planing A dental procedure in which the surfaces of the tooth root are smoothed.

sanitize To make clean; to free of bacteria and other germs.

scaler An instrument used for scraping deposits from teeth.

tartar Also called calculus, a hard deposit that forms on teeth. It is composed of plaque and minerals, especially calcium.

therapeutic Designed to heal.

for more information

American Academy of Pediatric Dentistry (AAPD)
211 East Chicago Avenue, Suite 1700
Chicago, IL 60611-2637
(312) 337-2169
Web site: http://www.aapd.org
This is an organization of dentists who specialize in children's
    dentistry. Although geared to its members, the academy
    has a number of brochures and other publications with
    information on aspects of oral health for children.

American Dental Association (ADA)
211 East Chicago Avenue
Chicago, IL 60611-2678
(312) 440-2500
Web site: http://www.ada.org
This professional society of dentists provides information and
    resources about oral health to dentists and the general
    public.

American Dental Hygienists Association (ADHA)
444 North Michigan Avenue, Suite 3400
Chicago, IL 60611
(312) 440-8900
Web site: http://www.adha.org
The American Dental Hygienists Association is a professional
    organization of dental hygienists providing information
    and publications about the practice of dental hygiene.

Bureau of Labor Statistics (BLS)
U.S. Department of Labor

2 Massachusetts Avenue NE, Suite 2135
Washington, DC 20212-0001
(202) 691-5700
Web site: http://www.bls.gov
Every year, the BLS updates the *Occupational Outlook Handbook*, which describes thousands of careers with details about job requirements and average salaries.

Canadian Dental Hygienist Association (CDHA)
96 Centrepointe Drive
Ottawa, ON K2G 6B1
Canada
(800) 267-5235 and (613) 224-5515
Web site: http://www.cdha.ca
The Canadian Dental Hygienist Association provides information and resources about oral health to dentists and the general public.

Commission on Dental Accreditation, American Dental Association
211 East Chicago Avenue
Chicago, IL 60611
Web site: http://www.ada.org/117.aspx
This organization provides information about accredited programs and educational requirements.

Commission on Dental Accreditation of Canada (CDA)
1815 Alta Vista Drive
Ottawa, ON K1G 3Y6
Canada
(613) 523-7114 and (866) 521-2322
Web site: http://www.cda-adc.ca
The commission accredits dental education programs throughout Canada. It provides information on accreditation requirements and accredited programs.

Dr. Samuel D. Harris National Museum of Dentistry
31 South Greene Street
Baltimore, MD 21201
(410) 706-0600
Web site: http://www.dentalmuseum.org
Affiliated with the Smithsonian Institution, this museum has
    entertaining and educational exhibits, a traveling program,
    and interactive information on its Web site that teaches
    children about healthy choices and habits that promote
    dental health.

WEB SITES

Due to the changing nature of Internet links, Rosen Publishing
has developed an online list of Web sites related to the subject
of this book. This site is updated regularly. Please use this link
to access the list:

http://www.rosenlinks.com/ECAR/DHY

for further reading

Aulie, Nancy. *Career Diary of a Dental Hygienist: Thirty Days Behind the Scenes with a Professional.* Herndon, VA: Garth Gardner, 2007.

Baker, Eric W., ed. *Head and Neck Anatomy for Dental Medicine.* New York, NY: Thieme Medical Publishers, 2010.

Chandra, Deborah, and Madeleine Comora. *George Washington's Teeth.* New York, NY: Farrar, Straus and Giroux, 2003.

Fehrenbach, Margaret, and Susan W. Herring. *Illustrated Anatomy of the Head and Neck.* 4th ed. St. Louis, MO: Elsevier Saunders, 2012.

Freitag, Jamie M. *Confessions of a Perio Princess: What They Didn't Teach You in Dental Hygiene School.* Seattle, WA: CreateSpace, 2010.

Iannucci, Joen M., and Laura Janse Howerton. *Dental Radiography: Principles and Techniques.* 4th ed. St. Louis, MO: Elsevier Saunders, 2012.

Kachlany, Scott C. *Infectious Disease of the Mouth* (Deadly Diseases & Epidemics). New York, NY: Chelsea House Publishers, 2007.

Kendall, Bonnie. *Opportunities in Dental Careers.* New York, NY: McGraw-Hill, 2006.

Libal, Autumn, Christopher Hovius, and Mary Ann McDonnell. *Taking Care of Your Smile: A Teen's Guide to Dental Care.* Broomall, PA: Mason Crest Publishers, 2005.

Morkes, Andrew. *Hot Health Care Careers: More Than 25 Cutting-Edge Occupations with the Fastest Growth and Most New Positions.* Chicago, IL: College & Career Press, 2011.

Newby, Cynthia. *Computers in the Dental Office.* Student Text with Data Disk. New York, NY: McGraw-Hill, 2005.

Porterfield, Jason. *Your Career in the Army* (The Call of Duty: Careers in the Armed Forces). New York, NY: Rosen Publishing, 2012.

Siegal, Jay. *Forensic Science at Work* (Contemporary Issues). New York, NY: Rosen Publishing, 2011.

Somervill, Barbara. *Dental Hygienist* (Cool Careers). Ann Arbor, MI: Cherry Lake Publishing, 2011.

Strange, Cordelia. *Medical Technicians: Health-Care Support for the 21st Century* (New Careers for the 21st Century: Finding Your Role in the Global Renewal). Broomall, PA: Mason Crest Publishers, 2010.

Tomko, Paula. *National Dental Hygienist Licensure Exam.* 3rd ed. New York, NY: Kaplan Publishing, 2009.

Wilkins, Esther M. *Clinical Practice of the Dental Hygienist.* 10th ed. Philadelphia, PA: Lippincott Williams & Wilkins, 2009.

Winchester, Elizabeth. *The Right Bite: Dentists as Detectives* (24/7: Science Behind the Scenes: Forensics). New York, NY: Scholastic, 2007.

bibliography

American Dental Association. "National Board Dental Examinations, Sample Test." Retrieved January 24, 2012 (http://www.ada.org/sections/educationAndCareers/pdfs/nbdhe_sample_test.pdf).

American Dental Hygienists' Association. *Dental Hygiene Education Facts: Curricula, Program and Graduate Information.* Chicago, IL: American Dental Hygienists' Association, 2011.

American Dental Hygienists' Association. *Survey of Dental Hygienists in the United States, 2007: Executive Summary.* Albany, NY: Center for Health Workforce Studies at the School of Public Health, University at Albany (the Center) for the American Dental Hygienists' Association, 2009.

American Dental Hygienists' Association. *Working* (Stories of Judy Boothby, Tonya Ray). Retrieved December 1, 2011 (http://www.adha.org/publications/working).

Charles, Christine H., and Maryann Cugini. "Research as a Career Option for Dental Hygienists," *Access,* Vol. 20, No. 9, November 2006, pp. 27–31.

Grant, Alexis. "The 50 Best Careers." *U.S. News and World Report,* December 6, 2010. Retrieved January 28, 2012 (http://money.usnews.com/money/careers/articles/2010/12/06/the-50-best-careers-of-2011).

Joint Commission on National Dental Examinations. *National Board National Dental Hygiene Examination.* Retrieved January 25, 2012 (http://www.ada.org/2662.aspx).

Psychological Services Bureau. *Sample Questions for the PSB Health Occupations Aptitude Examination.* Retrieved

January 24, 2012 (http://admin.psbtests.com/Uploads/
SiteResources/11HOAEsq.pdf).

U.S. Bureau of Labor Statistics. "Dental Hygienists."
Occupational Outlook Handbook, 2010–2011 Edition.
Retrieved November 29, 2011 (http://www.bls.gov/oco/
ocos097.htm#emply).

WebMD. "Dental X-Rays" 2010. Retrieved January 12, 2012
(http://www.webmd.com/oral-health/dental-x-rays).

Zayan, Meg. "History of Dental Hygiene." *Connecticut
Dental Hygienist Association*, 2011. Retrieved
January 2, 2011 (http://www.cdha-rdh.com/home/
historyofdentalhygiene.html).

index

ABOUT THE AUTHOR

A youth worker, writer, and editor, Ann Byers has written, among others, books that help young people find jobs in today's challenging career market. They include *Great Résumé, Application, and Interview Skills* and *Jobs as Green Builders and Planners.*

PHOTO CREDITS

Cover © iStockphoto.com/Stígur Karlsson; cover (background), p. 1 © iStockphoto.com/d_michel; pp. 4, 56-57 MCT/Getty Images; pp. 8–9 Fuse/Getty Images; pp. 10–11 Highforge Solutions/Shutterstock.com; pp. 16–17 © Los Angeles Daily News/ZUMA Press; pp. 18–19 © Richard Sennott/Star Tribune/ZUMA Press; p. 21 David Trotman-Wilkins/KRT/ Newscom; pp. 24–25 Kristyna Wentz-Graff/MCT/Landov; pp. 28–29 Huntstock/Getty Images; p. 30 Universal Images Group/Getty Images; pp. 32–33 Richard Hutchings/Photo Researchers/Getty Images; pp. 34–35 © David Crane/Los Angeles Daily News/ZUMA Press; pp. 38–39 Skip Nall/ Photodisc/Getty Images; p. 41 © Augusta Chronicle/ZUMA Press; pp. 44–45 Barry Williams/Getty Images; pp. 48–49 iStockphoto/Thinkstock; pp. 50, 51 © AP Images; pp. 52–53 © Belinda Images/SuperStock; pp. 60–61 Medioimages/ Photodisc/Getty Images; pp. 66–67 Purestock/Thinkstock.

Designer: Matt Cauli; Editor: Kathy Kuhtz Campbell; Photo Researcher: Amy Feinberg